Plastics

Edited by Rebecca Stefoff

Text © 1990 by Garrett Educational Corporation
First Published in the United States in 1990
by Garrett Educational Corporation,
130 E. 13th Street, Ada, OK 74820

First Published 1989 by A&C Black (Publishers) Limited, London
with the title PLASTICS
1989 © A&C Black (Publishers) Ltd.

Library of Congress Cataloging-in-Publication Data

Cash, Terry.
    Plastics / Terry Cash ; photographs by Ed Barber.
    p. cm. - (Threads)
    Includes index.
    Summary: Describes how plastics are made into many different
products from bottles and bags to tubes and toys. Includes ideas for a variety
of simple projects and experiments.
    ISBN 0-944483-70-4
    1. Plastics-Juvenile literature. [1. Plastics. 2. Plastics-Experiments.
3. Experiments.] I. Barber, Ed, ill. II. Title. III. Series.
TP1125.C376   1990
668.4-dc20
                          90-40368
                            CIP
                            AC

Plastics

Terry Cash

Photographs by Ed Barber

Contents

GEC **GARRETT EDUCATIONAL CORPORATION**

How do you use plastics?

Almost everything that you use has some plastic in it.

I'm eating from a plastic container.

This bag is plastic.

What would happen if all the plastics in your home and school disappeared overnight? What materials could you use instead of plastics?

My glasses are made from plastic.

This plant is growing in a plastic flowerpot.

I'm measuring with a plastic jar.

3

4

Collecting and sorting plastics

How many different kinds of plastic can you collect?

Some plastic things, such as saucepan handles, are tough and strong. Others, such as food wrappers or shopping bags, are thin and papery.

Many plastics are brightly colored, but some are white or even transparent. Some plastics, such as nylon, can be made into threads and woven into fabric for clothes.

How will you sort out your collection? Into groups like this?

How many other ways of sorting and grouping can you find?

Testing plastics

Different kinds of plastic have different jobs to do. You can do some simple tests to find out more about the plastics in your collection.

Try bending the plastic. Does it bend easily, or is it very difficult to make it change shape? Saucepan handles wouldn't be of much use if they were made out of the soft, flexible plastic used for dishwashing soap bottles. ▶

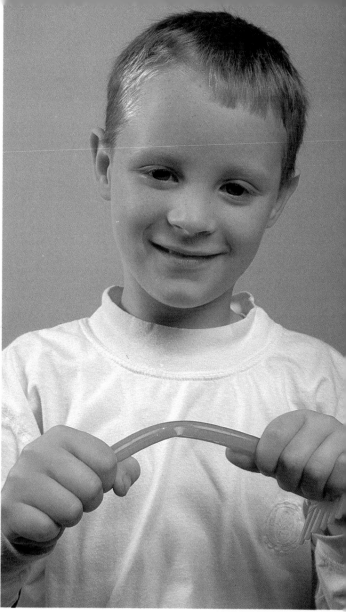

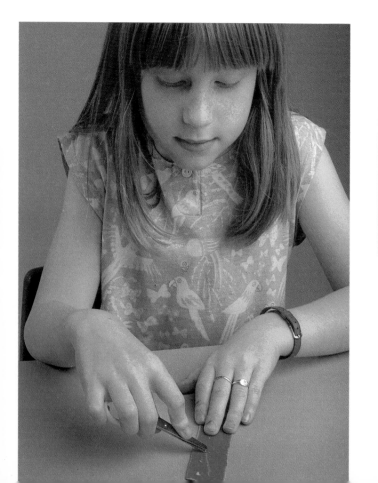

◀ Try scratching the plastic with your thumbnail. If this doesn't work, try using a pair of scissors. Soft plastics will mark quite easily; some are much harder. If plastic table tops or the lenses of glasses scratched easily, they would be ruined very quickly.

How many things in your collection will float on water? Fill a large bowl or tank with water and put your plastic objects into the water one at a time. Before you put each object into the water, guess whether it will float or sink. Did you guess correctly?

Will an empty plastic bottle float? Do you think a bottle full of water will float?

From oil to plastics

Most plastics are made from chemicals that come from oil. Each type of plastic (such as nylon or polythene) is made from different chemicals. A chemical factory turns the oil into plastic granules, like the ones around the edge of this page.

Most plastics have no color of their own, so colored dyes are added. Can you see the pieces of blue dye mixed in with these white plastic granules?

The plastic granules are delivered to factories that make plastic products, such as bottles or bags. There are lots of different ways to make plastic products, but they all have one thing in common. The plastic is heated until it becomes soft and runny, like syrup. Then it can be made into different shapes. When the plastic cools down, it sets and keeps its new shape.

Some plastics can be shaped only once, but others can change their shape if they are heated again.

How bags are made

Bags are made from plastic that has been heated and rolled into thin sheets by machines with big, heavy metal rollers.

It's just like rolling out modeling clay or dough with a rolling pin. Can you roll out a sheet of clay as thin as a plastic bag?

①

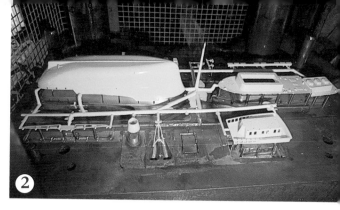

②

Making molds

Most plastic things are shaped inside molds. The mold is made to look like the outside of the product.

1. This is the mold for a toy boat.

2. The soft plastic is poured into the mold. When the plastic cools, it takes on the shape of the boat.

Would you like to try making your own mold?

You will need

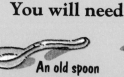
An old spoon

Modeling clay

A small bowl

Some water

Plaster of paris

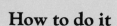
Tree bark (or another interesting shape)

How to do it

Press the modeling clay onto the bark and carefully peel it off again. You will find the bark's pattern in the clay. This is like a mold. Now mix some plaster of paris with water and pour it into your mold. When the plaster of paris sets, it will look like the tree bark pattern.

How bottles are made

Plastic bottles are made inside molds like the one in the picture. The mold is made to look like the outside of the bottle. Bottle molds are often made in two halves, so that the mold can be opened to take out the bottle. If soft plastic is blown up in the mold and then allowed to cool, it takes on the shape of the mold. This is called blow molding.

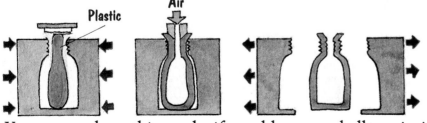

You can see how this works if you blow up a balloon inside a plastic pail or flowerpot. As the balloon swells, it takes on the shape of the pot. It fits the sides so closely that you can lift the pot just by holding the end of the balloon.

How containers are made

Plastic containers are made by squeezing, or injecting, the soft plastic through a narrow tube. This is called injection molding.

Containers, pails, and washbasins are made this way. Look at the bottom of a container or basin. In the middle you may see a small bump where the plastic has been cut from the end of the tube that squirted it into the mold. Can you see this bump in the photograph?

12

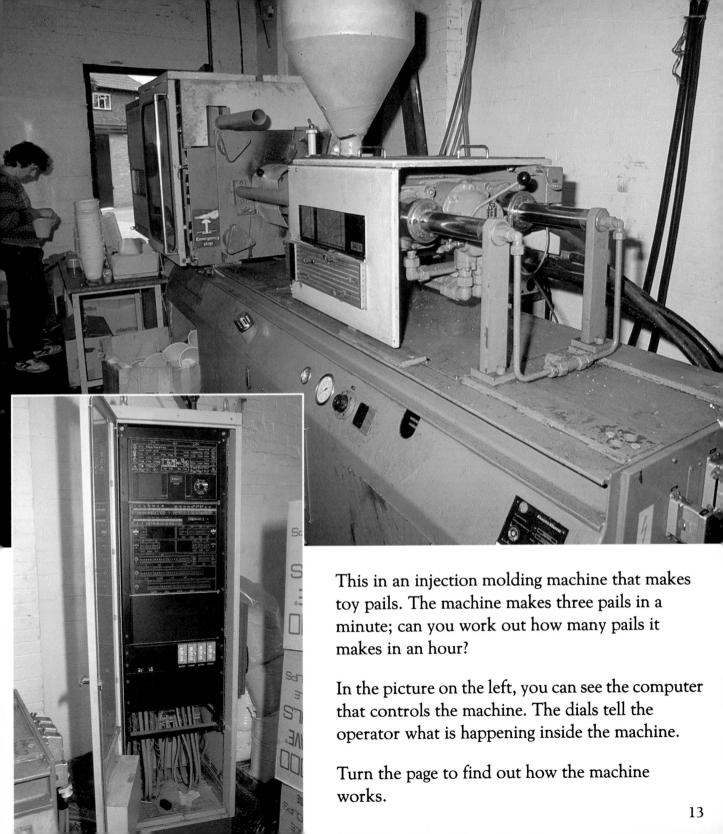

This in an injection molding machine that makes toy pails. The machine makes three pails in a minute; can you work out how many pails it makes in an hour?

In the picture on the left, you can see the computer that controls the machine. The dials tell the operator what is happening inside the machine.

Turn the page to find out how the machine works.

13

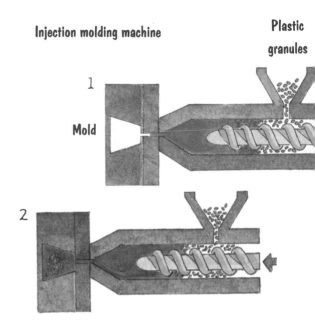

The drawings show you what an injection molding machine looks like inside. The photographs show what it looks like from the outside.

1. First, plastic granules are fed into the machine through a big funnel. Inside the machine, the granules are heated until they melt.

2. In the photograph, can you see the marks inside the mold? These marks make the patterns on the sides of the pail. The liquid plastic is pushed (injected) into the mold.

Ice-cold water around the mold cools the plastic so that it sets in the shape of a pail. When the plastic is cool, the mold opens and the pail falls out of the machine.

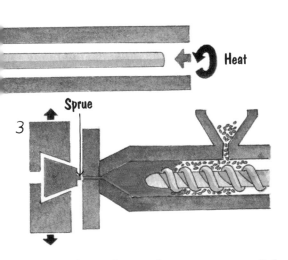

Heat

Sprue

3

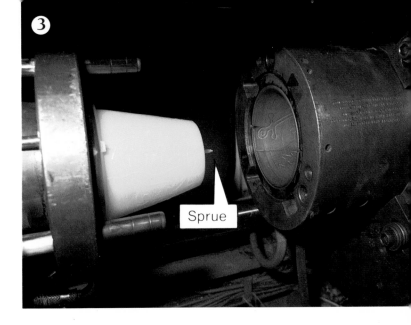

Sprue

3. When the pail comes out of the machine, it has a stalk called a sprue joined to the bottom. This is the plastic that was in the narrow tube that squirted plastic into the mold. On the front cover of this book, you can see lots of these sprues.

4. This man's job is to cut the sprues off the bottom of the pails.

Finally, handles have to be put on the pails. The finished pails are then packed in boxes and taken to stores by trucks.

New plastics from old

In the toy factory, the sprues and other waste plastic can be used again. First the waste plastic is sorted into different colors and types. Then it is put into a machine like this one.

Inside the machine, these sharp steel blades chop up the plastic into small pieces.

The pieces of old plastic are mixed with new plastic granules and used to make more toys.

How egg boxes are made

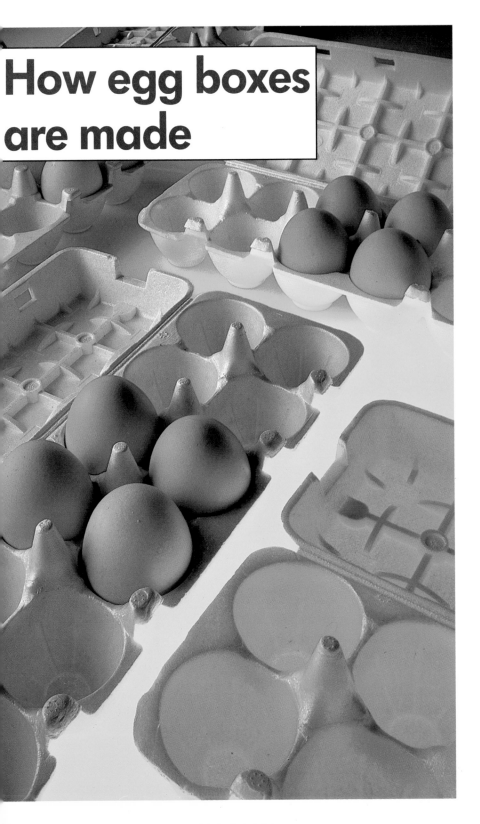

Shapes such as egg cartons are made by sucking a sheet of warm, soft plastic into a mold, like this.

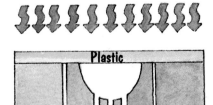

Heat

Plastic

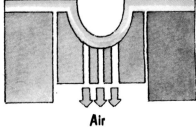

Air

When the plastic cools, it takes on the shape of the mold. This is called vacuum forming.

Look in a mirror and, with your lips tightly shut, suck in hard. You will see that your cheeks are pulled in against your jaws in the same way that the plastic sheet is sucked into the mold.

How pipes and tubes are made

Pipes, rods, and tubes are made by squeezing hot plastic through small holes. You can see how this is done if you squeeze cake icing out of the end of an icing bag. (Ask an adult to help you make the icing.)

Try squeezing the icing through different shaped nozzles. What shapes do you get? Can you match the lettered shapes with the numbered nozzles?

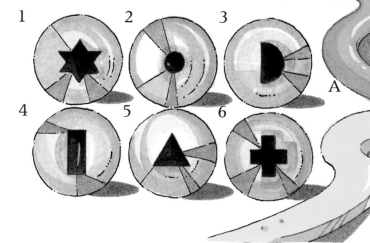

18

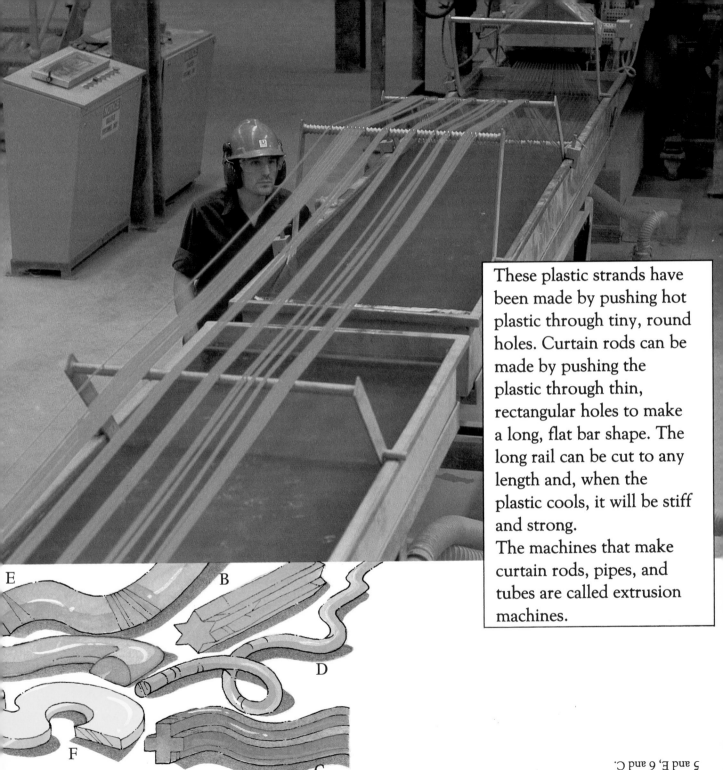

These plastic strands have been made by pushing hot plastic through tiny, round holes. Curtain rods can be made by pushing the plastic through thin, rectangular holes to make a long, flat bar shape. The long rail can be cut to any length and, when the plastic cools, it will be stiff and strong.

The machines that make curtain rods, pipes, and tubes are called extrusion machines.

E

B

D

F

C

The answers are upside down at the bottom of this page.

These nozzles and shapes go together:
1 and B, 2 and D, 3 and A, 4 and F,
5 and E, 6 and C.

19

Plastics for clothes

Some special plastics can be squeezed through tiny holes so they come out as fine, strong threads. These threads can be woven into material for clothes.
Look at the labels inside your clothes. Can you find any labels that say nylon or polyester? These are plastics.

See if you can find a pair of socks made from nylon and another pair made from a natural fiber, such as cotton. Put a cotton sock on one foot and a nylon sock on the other foot and run about for a little while. Which sock feels more comfortable? In hot weather, would you prefer to wear a cotton sock or a nylon sock?

How strong are plastics?

Have you ever helped carry the groceries and found that the handle of the bag has snapped or the bottom of the bag is torn? Are plastic bags stronger than paper ones? Can you think of a fair test to find the strongest shopping bag?

Do plastics keep things warm?

Materials that keep warm things warm (and cold things cold) are called insulators. Try this test to see if plastics are better insulators than natural materials.

You will need

Something made from cotton

Rubber bands

Something made from polyester

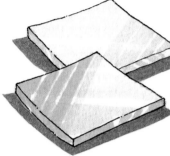

A piece of plastic foam (ceiling tiles and packing materials are often made from this)

5 plastic cups (make sure they are all the same size and shape)

Lots of ice cubes

Something made from wool

How to do it

1. Put the same number of ice cubes into each cup. Wrap one cup in wool, one in cotton, one in polyester, and one in plastic foam. Use the rubber bands to hold the materials around the cups.

It doesn't matter what order you do this in as long as you leave one cup open and unwrapped.

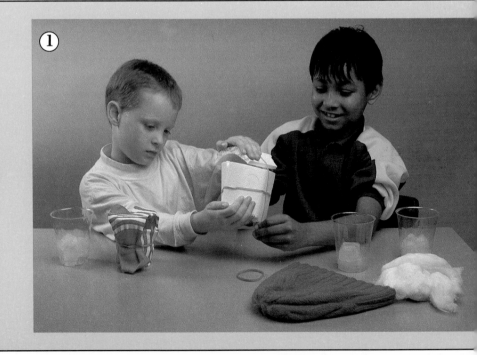

①

2. When the ice in the open cup has melted, unwrap the other cups. What do you think you will find? Do you think that the cloth has warmed the ice and melted it? Or have you discovered that it stops the cold from escaping and keeps the ice solid? Which material keeps the ice solid the longest? This one is the best insulator.

Plastics and the environment

If you tried the tests to compare plastic bags with paper bags, you may have found that paper bags fall apart much more easily than do plastic ones. But the strength of plastic bags is not always a good thing.

Bury some plastic objects in the ground next to some paper and cardboard. Mark the spot. After a few weeks, dig everything up again. You will find that the paper and cardboard is beginning to decay, or decompose, but the plastic is as good as new. Plastic garbage is very hard to get rid of. This is one reason why scientists are trying to make new kinds of plastic that will break up and decay.

Plastics are very useful because they can be made into so many different products and they last a long time. But what will happen to all the plastic trash you throw away every day?

More things to do

1. Which are the best materials to wear in the rain? Can you think of a clever way of testing clothes to see how waterproof they are? Once they have soaked through, which materials dry fastest—manmade plastic materials such as nylon, or natural ones such as wool and cotton?

2. Which do you think are the most comfortable pillows, those filled with feathers or those filled with plastic foam? Do a survey to find out what the rest of your class thinks when they try two different kinds of pillows.

3. Expanded polystyrene is the name of the plastic foam that meat trays, fast-food containers, and ceiling tiles are made from. It is very light and floats well. How much weight can a small piece hold before it sinks? Does it float better than wood? Does it float higher in water than cork?

4. Some wallpaper has a thin plastic coating called vinyl. If it gets dirty, you can wipe it clean with a damp cloth. This can be helpful, but why will it be a problem when you need to strip the wall to put up new paper?

5. Make a list of things that were once made from glass and are now made from plastic. Which do you think is better—plastic or glass? Why? What other materials has plastic replaced?

6. Plastic bottles have to take quite a pounding when they get bumped, dropped, or banged. Can you think of a way of testing different bottles to see which ones are the strongest?

7. Imagine a world without plastics. What natural things could you use instead? Shoes were once made from leather—now many are plastic. Do plastic shoes last longer than leather ones? How can you find out?

8. Are eggs better protected in cardboard egg cartons or in plastic ones?

9. Try rubbing something plastic, such as a comb, plastic pen, or bottle, against your sweater. Then hold the object near your hair. What happens? Find out what happens after 10 rubs and after 20 rubs. Does this happen with objects made from wood, paper, or other materials?

Index